CLOTHING

Eco Activities

Written by
Louise Nelson

CRABTREE
PUBLISHING COMPANY
WWW.CRABTREEBOOKS.COM

CRABTREE
PUBLISHING COMPANY
WWW.CRABTREEBOOKS.COM

Author: Louise Nelson

Editorial Director: Kathy Middleton

Editors: Robin Twiddy, Ellen Rodger

Proofreader: Crystal Sikkens

Cover/Interior Design: Jasmine Pointer

Production coordinator and

Prepress technician: Margaret Amy Salter

Print coordinator: Katherine Berti

Photo Credits

All images are courtesy of Shutterstock.com, unless otherwise specified. With thanks to Getty Images, Thinkstock Photo and iStockphoto. Paper Texture Throughout – Borja Andreu. Front Cover – elenabsl, Olga1818, Africa Studio, Olga Kovalenko, BonNontawat, Topuria Design. 4–5 – Ernest Rose, Catherine Zibo, Mark Nazh, Air Images. 6–7 – Vadim Zakharishchev, Andrienko Anastasiya, FX Andy, Cherkas, Petinov Sergey Mihilovich. 8–9 – Zonicboom, Yuriy Golub, New Africa, Lubava, nikkytok. 10–11 – Olga Kovalska, Accurate shot, titosart, Qualivity, xMarshall, Terdpong, Lunatictm. 12–13 – Shnarf, Sarycheva Olesia, Vasilius, Elena Schweitzer. 14–15 – Cryptographer, Aleksandar Todorovic, Vuk Varuna, Odua Images, melaics. 16–17 – TY Lim, saltodemata, wavebreakmedia, Air Images. 18–19 – MongPro, Danilaleo, stormur, MyImages – Micha, pukach, oksana2010, Nonnakrit. 20–21 – Hein Nouwens, Creative Stall, Suphatthra olovedog, Marius GODOI, ms.nen. 22–23 – Vitaliya, anastasiia agafonova, David Tadevosian, SunCity, Margarita R. Padilla, y Hurst Photo, Alina G.

Library and Achives Canada Cataloguing in Publication

Title: Clothing : eco activities / written by Louise Nelson.
Names: Nelson, Louise, 1981- author.
Description: Includes index.
Identifiers: Canadiana (print) 20200356836 | Canadiana (ebook) 20200356844 |
   ISBN 9781427128607 (hardcover) |
   ISBN 9781427128645 (softcover) |
   ISBN 9781427128683 (HTML)
Subjects: LCSH: Textile crafts—Juvenile literature. | LCSH: Clothing and dress—
   Recycling—Juvenile literature. | LCSH: Refuse as art material—Juvenile
   literature. | LCSH: Handicraft—Juvenile literature.
Classification: LCC TT699 .N45 2021 | j746—dc23

Library of Congress Cataloging-in-Publication Data

Names: Nelson, Louise, author.
Title: Clothing eco activities / Louise Nelson.
Description: New York, NY : Crabtree Publishing Company, 2021. |
   Series: Eco activities | Includes index.
Identifiers: LCCN 2020045621 (print) | LCCN 2020045622 (ebook) |
   ISBN 9781427128607 (hardcover) |
   ISBN 9781427128645 (paperback) |
   ISBN 9781427128683 (ebook)
Subjects: LCSH: Clothing trade--Juvenile literature. | Clothing trade--
   Environmental aspects--Juvenile literature. | Recycling industry--Juvenile
   literature. | Refuse and refuse disposal--Juvenile literature.
Classification: LCC TD195.T48 N45 2021 (print) | LCC TD195.T48 (ebook) |
   DDC 628.4/458--dc23
LC record available at https://lccn.loc.gov/2020045621
LC ebook record available at https://lccn.loc.gov/2020045622

Crabtree Publishing Company

www.crabtreebooks.com   1-800-387-7650
Published by Crabtree Publishing Company in 2021

Printed in the U.S.A./122020/CG20201014

Published in Canada
Crabtree Publishing
616 Welland Avenue
St. Catharines, Ontario
L2M 5V6

Published in the United States
Crabtree Publishing
347 Fifth Ave
Suite 1402-145
New York, NY 10016

CONTENTS

Page 4   A Clothing Crisis

Page 6   What Are Textiles?

Page 8   Crafty Kicks

Page 12   A Well-dressed Garden

Page 16   Fast Fashion Frenzy

Page 18   The Bum Bag

Page 22   Make Do and Mend

Page 24   Glossary and Index

Words that are **bolded** can be found in the glossary on page 24.

A CLOTHING CRISIS

Stop before you shop! We are buying more new clothes than ever before. This means we're throwing away more clothes than ever before, too.

Did you know?
Many of the things we throw away can be used again for something else.

About 80 billion pieces of clothing are bought by people throughtout the world each year. Clothes are then thrown away when people think they are old, ruined, or out of style. But what can we do instead?

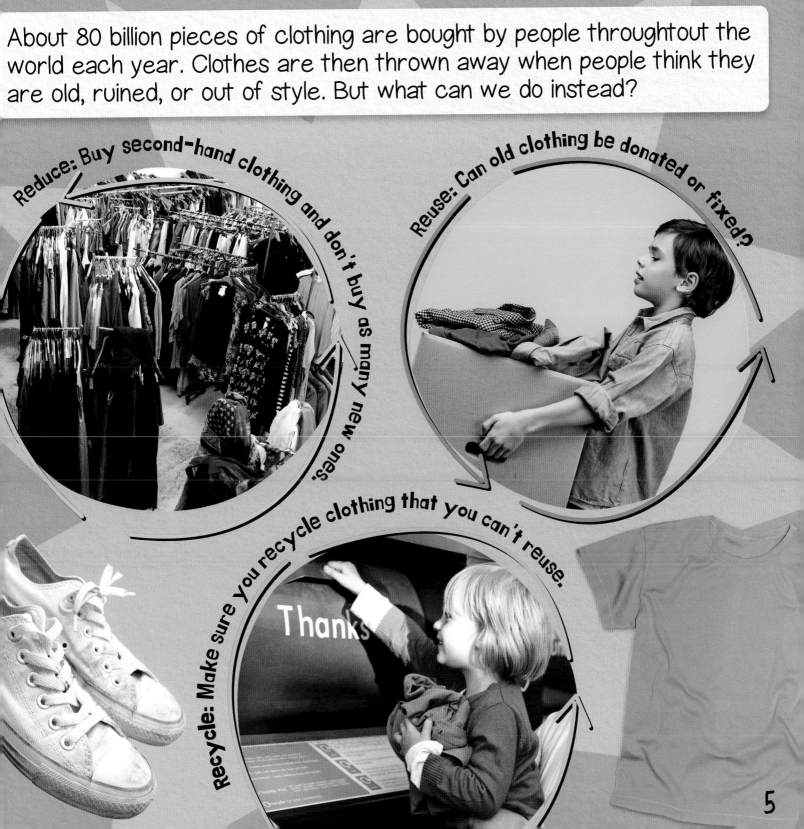

Reduce: Buy second-hand clothing and don't buy as many new ones.

Reuse: Can old clothing be donated or fixed?

Recycle: Make sure you recycle clothing that you can't reuse.

Thanks

WHAT ARE TEXTILES?

Textiles are materials that are made up of **threads**. We use different materials, such as wood, glass, paper, and metal, to make all kinds of things. Materials have properties. Properties tell us what the material is like.

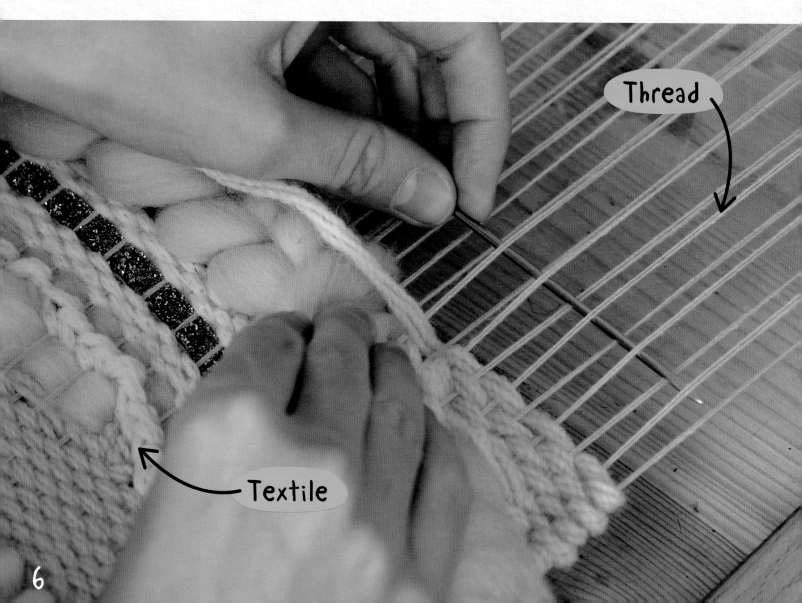

Thread

Textile

The Properties of Textiles

Can be natural or synthetic

Flexible

Different textiles have different properties.

Can be soft or rough

CRAFTY KICKS

Are your sneakers less white than they used to be? Don't throw them away if they're going gray. Give them a new life instead!

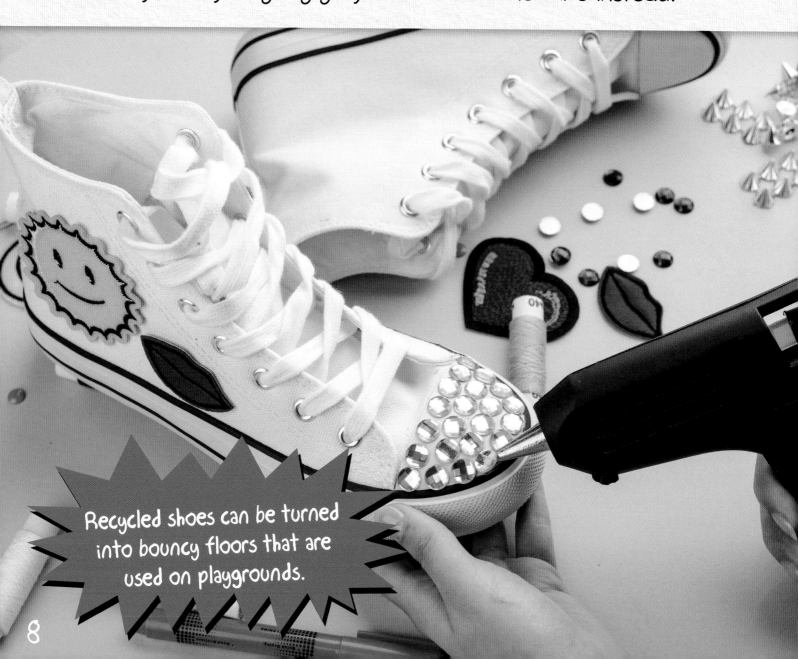

Recycled shoes can be turned into bouncy floors that are used on playgrounds.

You will need:

- Old shoes
- Glue (fabric glue or hot glue gun)
- Gems, charms, and patches
- Fabric paint or markers

Safety First!

Hot glue guns can burn. Only use these with an adult.

Make sure your shoes are clean and dry.

Use the glue to add gems and patches to the shoes.

STEP 3. Use fabric markers to draw pictures and patterns onto your shoes.

STEP 4. Let them dry.

Don't wear your creations outside if it's wet!

11

A WELL-DRESSED GARDEN

You love dressing up. Why not dress up your plants too?

Can you make a scarecrow from old clothing?

You will need:

- Plants in pots
- Old clothes and boots

Clean as You Go

Remember to wear gardening gloves when working with plants and soil.

If you use your imagination, old boots and clothing can make very nice plant pots.

These old boots look pretty when used as flowerpots.

Hang them up for a cool display.

Just chilling in the sunshine.

Old clothes that are too worn to wear every day can be worn for messy activities, such as gardening. You won't mind getting your old clothes muddy!

FAST FASHION FRENZY

Clothing is cheaper than ever before. It might seem like a really good thing, but it means that people are making more clothes and throwing more away. This is bad for the **environment**.

Clothing like this does not last very long. They are often quickly thrown away.

There are some simple steps to take that can help!

- Mend clothing to make them last longer.

- Give clothing to charities and second-hand stores when you don't want them anymore.

- Make sure clothes are recycled when you can't use them anymore.

- When you can, buy your clothing at thrift stores.

- Buy clothing made from strong, natural materials.

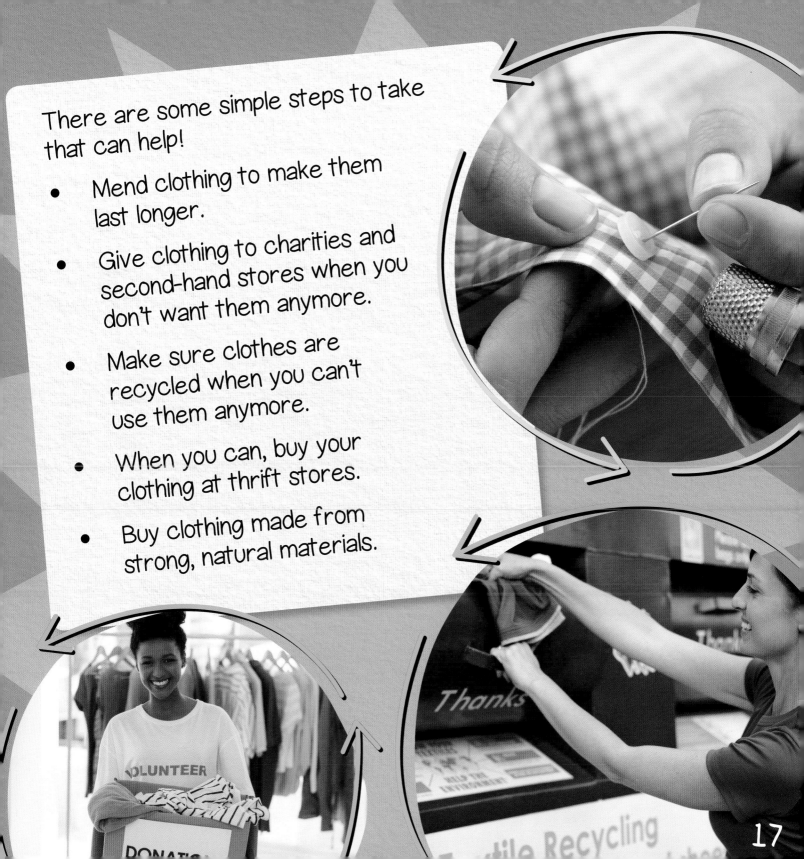

VOLUNTEER

DONATI

Thanks

Textile Recycling

THE BUM BAG

This bag is made from the back of an old pair of jeans. It's roomy and has many pockets. It's sure to jazz up any outfit!

Some textiles are made of plastic. If your clothing says "polyester" in the label, it's got plastic in it! Plastic is bad for the planet.

You will need:

- An old pair of jeans
- Fabric scissors
- Needle and thread or sewing machine
- Ribbons and other decorations
- Straight pins

Don't Forget!

Always have an adult help you with sewing machines.

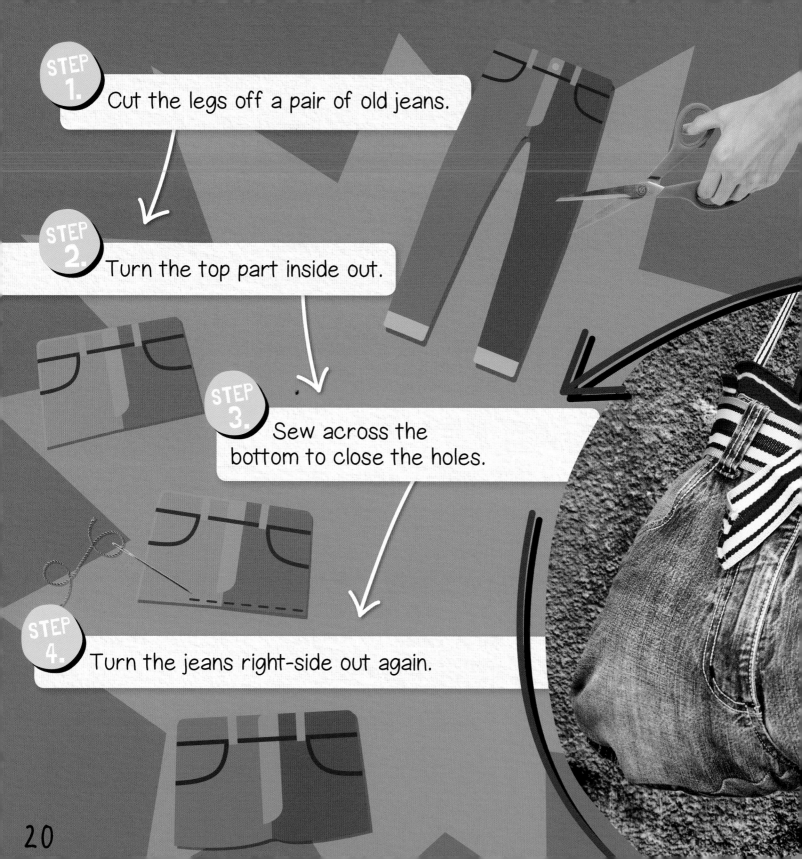

STEP 1. Cut the legs off a pair of old jeans.

STEP 2. Turn the top part inside out.

STEP 3. Sew across the bottom to close the holes.

STEP 4. Turn the jeans right-side out again.

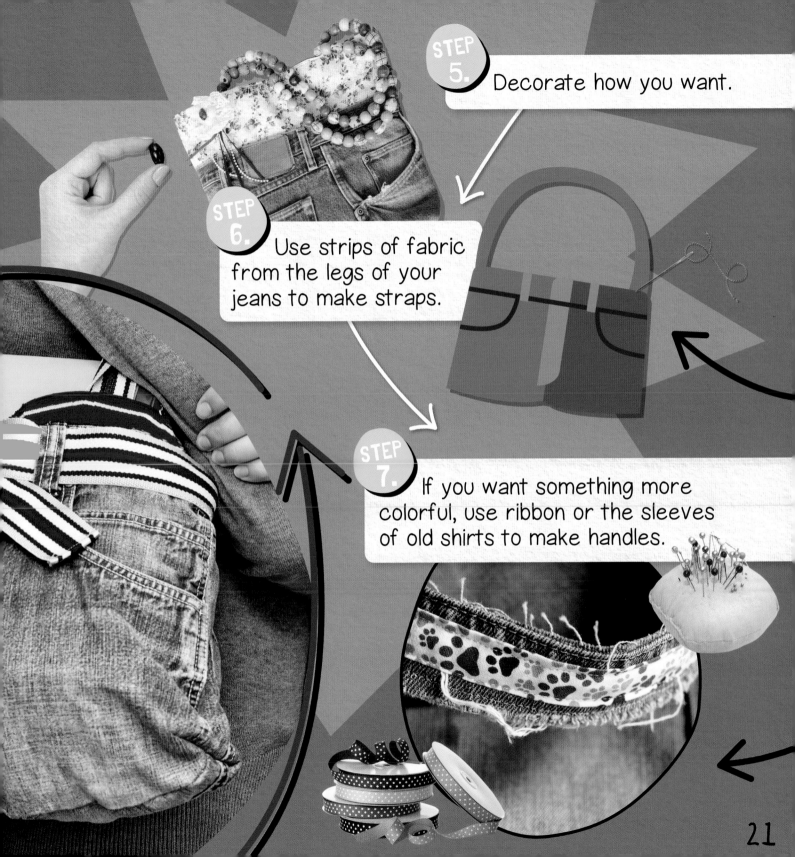

STEP 5. Decorate how you want.

STEP 6. Use strips of fabric from the legs of your jeans to make straps.

STEP 7. If you want something more colorful, use ribbon or the sleeves of old shirts to make handles.

21

MAKE DO AND MEND

Clothes will get holes in them, but don't throw them away! With a few simple sewing skills and a bit of creativity, you can turn old clothes into a dream outfit!

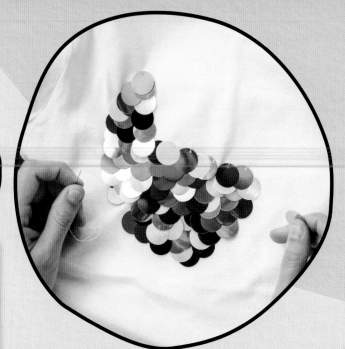

Sew colorful sequins over a spill or a stain.

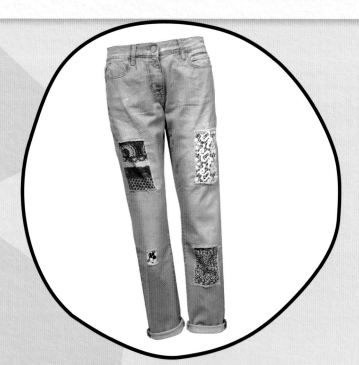

These colorful patches are made from old shirts.

Fabric paint can bring an old, faded T-shirt back to life!

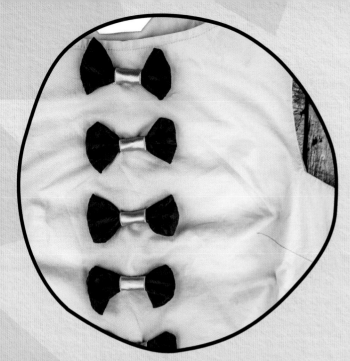

Sew ribbons onto an old dress
to make it fashionable again.

This skirt was made from two pairs
of old jeans! Can you see the legs?

Novelty buttons can
make an old shirt interesting.

Unravel old sweaters
and use the yarn again.

GLOSSARY

environment	The natural world
flexible	Easy to bend
natural	Found in nature and not made by people
novelty	New, different, original, or unusual
recycle	Use again to make something else
synthetic	Unnatural, made by people
threads	Thin strands of cotton, nylon, or other materials

INDEX

bags 18

gardens 12–13, 15

jeans 18–21, 23

plastic 18

playgrounds 8

properties 6–7

recycling 5, 8, 17

scarecrows 12

sewing 19–20, 22–23

shoes 8–11